Legions of Light
Armies of Darkness

Rick Smith
UFOteacher

This book is a work of non-fiction. Names and places have been changed to protect the privacy of all individuals. The events and situations are true.

First published by AuthorHouse 02/23/05

ISBN: 1-4107-9406-7 (e-book)
ISBN: 1-4184-4837-0 (Paperback)
ISBN: 1-4184-4838-9 (Dust Jacket)

Library of Congress Control Number: 2003096000

First Printing 1999
Second Printing 2003

This book is printed on acid free paper.

Printed in the United States of America
Bloomington, IN

Smith & Smyth Creations, LLC
Merrick, New York 11566 U.S.A.
www.SmithandSmyth.com

DEDICATED TO:

My family – Mom, Dad, Rob, Nancy, and the adventures of Isabelle and Sophia, 2 years old and 8 months old, respectively. They represent a new avenue in my life, one that has refueled my will to assault an ugly Orwellian present that I hope they never inherit.

My friends – past and present. For some, it has been easier for you to part ways... I understand. I go where angels dare not tread while you do as your demons tell you. For others, the convictions of your friendship and support have been irreplaceable in my life. I know it's a bitch to admit that you know me, especially since I have never mellowed with time.

Whether you faded into the past or remained in the present, all have served as a source of inspiration in one way or another to get the book written, designed, self-published and then, in final, *officially published in 2003.*

Last but not least – L. La Mermaid, Ruby Turtledove, J.M. Starchild and the Fantastic Four. Life was never the same after we met. This is a good thing... I have no regrets. The years have passed quickly since we last spoke – and so has the abyssal chasm of anguish left in its wake.

What remains is an equilibrium of happiness whenever a certain Aries or Capricorn comes to mind; thoughts that draw a wide smile and the tingling goose bumps of memories, reminding me in the mission of my own life's path that it was all good – even that dumbass shit at the end.

Now, somewhere out there on any given day, you may be shocked and amazed to come across this officially published version sitting on your bookstore's shelf. Furthermore, when you get past that 'shocked and amazed' part, you may feel compelled to pick the damn thing up and read what kind of senile lunacy I've committed this time. *'What the hell is he doing now?!?'*

If this should ever happen to you, then I want you to know something very important – *time heals all wounds.* And, regardless of where my life has ventured, *I miss you.* I always will.

Wherever your paths may take you, I wish you and the kids happiness and success in life. Somewhere in time, on any given day, we will cross paths again and I will be wearing a smile that says, *'Ah, there you are. Where have you been?'*

This will be a good thing… and I will have no regrets.

TABLE OF CONTENTS

PREFACE - 2003

It has taken the last four years to finally get my first book officially published. Evenso, this book, along with its forthcoming sequel, represents a focal point for the last ten years of experiences *here and abroad!* What this essentially means is three things:

- I have acheived what others said would never happen… and, to their shock and dismay, I will continue to acheive a lot more in the near future.

- What you may expect from this book, my art or my lectures is nothing compared to what you will actually get. If you ask me a question, you had better be prepared to get the answer. Otherwise, DON'T ASK as I have zero tolerance for other people's magnificent stupidity.

- The last ten years of my life have been a path less traveled with a very sordid venture of exploration, utilization and revelation, ranging from emotional and physical nirvana to that of a pure, untainted, USDA approved rag-ass bitch.

Being my own worst critic, I made it a point to review the contents of this book regularly and decided this time that the opportunity was apparent to include a preface, foreword and afterword for a second edition. Much of the original introduction has been left intact for accuracy, integrity and continuity so that the reader can understand where I was then as opposed to where I am now. The little anecdotes at the end of certain poems have also been left in for the same reason. Any parts that have been edited from the first edition are those that now reside in the preface, foreword, afterword or revised dedication page.

In any case, there have been some rather interesting social, political and human hurdles for me to surmount since I began this damned odyssey several years ago. Some of you may be stunned into a coma after reading this but the truth must come forth. Here are a few spiffy doodads that I picked up along the way:

• Contrary to popular myth, you cannot be taught anything by someone who has less than you. This will always come first as it sets the tone for every other spot of shmootz and pile of shmegma that you will cross swords with.

• Being out there on your own is the best way to accomplish your mission as a teacher of the masses, a civil rights leader or a social maverick. It is also the best way to find out who is with you in your karmic sphere of influence and who is against you. Remember, it is better to know who your enemies are before finding a friend. Friends may give you a platform of support but your enemies will always give you the stimulus, stamina, endurance and integrity you need to keep you focused and on your toes.

• Don't ever blindly join an organization or establishment just because you can. As one of the more assinine things you could do, it will diminish your integrity as a human being. The only people who ever find solace in these non-profit circus acts are simplistic imbeciles who never use more than one brain cell.

• Contrary to popular myth, human integrity far outweighs that bogus horseshit known as professional integrity. As with oil and water, human integrity requires infamy while professional integrity demands popularity. These two things shall never mix. I would like to thank all the useless and feeble imbeciles out there who had the nerve to call themselves my friend at some point in time. You see, I appreciate the fact that you went out of your way to eventually stab me in the back in order to satisfy that ego trip you call professional integrity. What didn't kill me only made me stronger — *and much more dangerous* to you and your shallow, self-serving allegiance to Repto-Sirian Fascism.

• It is unfortunate that my counterparts in the metaphysical, ufological and academic arenas of science – including some of my own friends and acquaintances – have never understood the difference between infamy and popularity. Most of them don't have the brass ones to realize it even if they wanted to. After all, it is much easier to hide behind the masked delusion of professional integrity, which never existed in the first place. In this way, someone like me can be labelled an embarrassing liability, and therefore censored by those who should be standing shoulder to shoulder with me. Am I infamous? Yes. Am I relentless? Yes. What I know and say is unpopular? You bet your ass it is. Did you really think I would just go away simply because you closed ranks against me? Did you really think that your shallow metaphysical, paranormal, supernatural, horse-blinder jingoism would protect you from someone as self-reliant and self-empowered as me? You must be joking, right?

• There are some notable, factual and highly useful aspects in the general whole life/metaphysical studies. However, most of them reside in the areas of homeopathy and its clinically proven parental guardian – immunotherapy. Outside of that, the metaphysical and paranormal arenas are mainly comprised of a bunch of dickless wonders with no friggin' grasp whatsoever of how extraterrestrial intervention and your shitty paycheck are tied at the hip.

• Contrary to popular myth, the "New Age" is not a movement – it is an industry. This self-serving, uneducated bunch of egomaniacs can't even hang on to an intelligent, thought-provoking conversation without running for cover. When you have to hide all of your sweet smelling bullshit behind a veil of corporate Repto-Sirian propaganda, you leave yourself wide open to hypocrisy, bigotry and suspicion as absolute power corrupts absolutely. Folks, the Black Panthers were a movement. If it doesn't compare to the Black Panthers then it doesn't make the grade... end of story!

• Conspiratorial freaks need to be shot dead on sight. The amount of time they spend digging up the infantile, vacuum-sealed crap they find leaves me wondering why the good guys from the Alpha Quadrant don't just wash their hands of us completely. On top of that, what they dig up is so "yesterday" that you have to wonder if these paranoid little piss-ants ever heard of the Abduction Phenomenon, the Bill of Rights or the Old Kingdom of Egypt. When you ask these ignorant left-wing or right-wing dumbasses if they ever bothered to read the Constitution of the United States, they fall flat on their faces with no answer. Henceforth, if you remain ignorant of the bigger picture, you will always be a little slave to the system and will live with conspiracies coming around ever new corner you turn. Sucks for you – *just don't get in my way.*

• Contrary to popular myth, life for you, me and the next door neighbor *is* a bitched up conspiracy. So get a life! Join a gym! Lose some fucking weight! Most of you are too damn fat and lazy anyway (and yes, if you eat shit then you look like shit). Visit the Great Wall of China (and get some exercise)! Have lots of sex (and lose some more weight)! Find that infamous left turn at Albuquerque! The fact that we are even here is itself an abomination of Mother Earth's foreign policy. Your parents may have opted for an abortion had they known early on that they were spawning otherworldly hybrids instead of the average, dim-witted, uneducated couch potatoe. Earth has always been a Dachau breeding ground for human slaves. So pull your ragged, infested, disease ridden, unclean ass out of that shithole sewer you've been dwelling in and get out into the REAL WORLD!

• You can kiss all that bloated, romantic crap about Darwinism and Creationism goodbye. If you think I am wrong, then take a good long look at the great white pimp known as Corporate America and its bend over bitch – Suburban America.

• Contrary to popular myth, education is empowerment. Straight up, hands down, no contest. Enlightenment is slavery in a state of psychological denial – henceforth, disempowerment. Learn the difference between these two things and you will see what I am saying. If you are one of those pansy-ass freaks who thinks that all the entities, ghosts and aliens frolic in the dandelion patch all day with nothing better to do than to whisper a bunch of sweet smelling crap to you *and only you,* then you leave me no choice but to kick your teeth down your throat. Don't be a weak-minded, disempowered simpleton or I will have no choice but to treat you like the second class citizen *that you have already chosen to be.*

• As a teacher of the masses, I am a relentless truth machine completely intolerant of other people's stupidity. *'What the hell does he mean?'* It means I am one of two things: I am your best friend (human integrity) or your worst enemy (professional integrity). As your friend, I will go to the mat for you and show you how to empower yourself, take a stand and fight back. As your enemy... well, let's hope you are not one of those as you may have to move to another state before I am finished with you. Pull your head out of your ass and figure it out. I have no time for your simplistic, naive or selectively ignorant bullshit.

• Contrary to popular myth, blood is not thicker than water. Especially when you take into consideration that the 'waters of life' gave birth to your non-indigenous family bloodline. The main point here is that you can choose your friends *and* your family. So do yourself and your loved ones a favor and cleave away the chaff and save the seed. Get rid of those ignorant, abusive assholes and useless, self-centered rejects. Don't need them. Don't want them. There is no reason at all for you or your loved ones to put up with the psychological, emotional or physical abuse that comes from years of dealing with these malignant jokers who never cared about you in the first place.

• Riddle me this folks: how could you ever hope to attain something called higher consciousness when your parents failed miserably at teaching you basic sentience? That's like flying a plane with no landing gear. Oh yeah, you'll soar really high up there. But eventually you are going to have to land somewhere. That's when you smack head first into the side of a nuclear missile silo housing a boatload of ugly historical truths you were never prepared to handle.

• Remember, your corporate masters have had about 500,000 years to manipulate and cajole the nuances of Humanity in there favor for the sake of fattening the financial revenues of the World Monetary Fund and the International Banking System. This, of course, feeds their bottom line profits in the Empire of Orion (aka: Ari-an, Aryan). What they can't get with vinegar (Judaism, Christianity, Islam) they'll get with honey (New Age Industry). Sorry folks, but you've been screwing yourselves over ever time you go to a church, temple, mosque or one of those mindless expos sponsored by the new age industry.

Get a grip, turn the boob-tube *off*, throw it out the damn window, read a book and learn about extraterrestrial patriarchal history and economic slavery as it is – not as you wish it to be for your own self-serving PT Barnum purposes. Your psychological denial leaves much to be desired, especially when I see ninety-five percent of the global population walking on their knees like indentured servants for some corporate, military-industrial, Repto-Sirian slug called God! And some of these low-class, no-talent asswipes actually have the nerve to wave ridiculous and baseless symbols of supposed freedom in the air while pledging their allegiance to some fictitious social fad called Democracy.

Do you still wonder why I have no tolerance for other people's stupidity?!? Shame on you. You're probably one of those disempowered jackasses who thinks 'president-select' George W. Bush is actually the elected President. Take yourself out to the pasture, do us all a favor and shoot yourself dead. An ignoramus like you does not deserve equal rights, especially since you wield your own selective ignorance like a mouthpiece of propaganda for the Overlords of Orion.

As you can tell, I no longer waste my time with the dumbass mentality of the metaphysical, new age industry as well as the delinquent NAZI academia of the conventional sciences and ufology.

As far as ufology, astrophysics, Egyptology and cosmology are concerned, they can basically bite my ruby red ass. I've had it with their self-serving shit.

These spineless pricks should rot in hell for the way they hide behind their Ph.D.'s (the infamous Pimpin' Ho's Degree) as some type of bureaucratic excuse to avoid ruining a preconceived, illogical and baseless notion of professional integrity.

WHAT IN FLAMING HELL DO YOU THINK YOU ARE PROTECTING?!?

Where I come from, there is no such thing as professional integrity as it amounts to little more than a fattened and lazy ego trip with no justification.

You see, you didn't get that degree from anything concerning xenobiology, xeno-archaeology or xeno-politics. How could you? Those fields of science, geo-politics and socio-economics, as well as other related fields of research, are as real as anything. However, what they are researching isn't supposed to exist in the first place. So how can you get a degree in something that doesn't exist, yet is funded by every government and corporate entity on the planet?

A Pimpin' Ho's Degree (Ph.D.) is meant for one thing only – to keep you in line with the established ministries of propaganda via other patented and controlled arenas of conventional academia that will never be allowed to think outside of the ordained shoebox mentality. So why would you let something like that control you? In the end of it all, your infantile perception of professional integrity is drastically flawed from top to bottom as the system has succeeded in taking something from you of much greater importance – human integrity!

Remember, when you are already dealing with the paranormal in an aggressive and proactive manner, your Ph.D. in whatever damn field you are coming from is automatically null and void. It was never meant to handle something that would lead to its own obsolescence. You crossed the line. Now shit or get off the pot and stop wasting my time with your self-serving intellectual egomania.

Malcolm, Martin, Christ, Harriet Tubman, Alexander the Great and a host of other men and women who came before me were willing to take a hit for the rest of us in order to disrupt the iron fist of economic slavery that holds sway over this planet. Now what the hell are you willing to do? Grow a pair of balls and get real.

Lastly, if there is one thing I am truly fed up with, it's all the delinquent disempowering rhetoric that sees a conspiracy around every corner. It's as if the reality of the situation has now become some sort of sociological excusal or psychological alibi for sitting on your ass and doing absolutely *nothing*. What the hell is that crap about?

Look folks, the fact that you are even born is itself the ultimate conspiracy. After all, the sole purpose of your existence is to serve the system like good, obedient automatons and worker ants. In this way, the mechanisms of reincarnation have become subject to the shallow and petty whimsy of historical patriarchal oppression for the last 500,000 years.

And you idiots act like there's something magnanimously new about some other useless little dingbat conspiracy you just tripped across by accident today. When did you plan on getting up off your ass and going after the actual historical issues that you've been ignoring with your own petty issues?

You see, liberation and self-empowerment can only come in one main form – the study of linguistics. The best and most accessible place for anyone to begin is with an unabridged English collegiate dictionary, also know as Linguistics 101. Using a comprehensive dictionary as a base to launch from, you'll be able go after Greek, Latin, Hebrew and Egyptian. If you want to free your mind and solve the Abduction Phenomenon once and for all, this is the way to go. But remember, this is also were things start to come full circle.

Ufologists would have to come to grips with the fact that the supreme God they've been worshipping alongside their scientific half-measures is one in the same with the corporate thug called Enlil, a tyrannical militant sadist who ruled over this kingdom (solar system) with an iron fist and set up shop here on Earth in what would come to be known as the Old Kingdom of Egypt.

The New Age industry would be exposed as the mouthpiece of propaganda that it is. Their rhetoric about going to the light is itself representative of the methods used by Enlil and his gumbah Annunaki henchmen to hunt down and brainwash our pre-homosapient ancestors with crystal technology. This technology and the caves that were rigged with such methods is what gave birth to the notion of 'going to the light' and having all your previous thoughts about freedom and independence replaced with mind-numbing obedience to the system (aka. Suburban America).

This method of luring and trapping people into collective, brainwashing congregations in private, selective caves (laboratories) became what we refer to as a church, temple, mosque, mystery school or secret societies, all of which require a high level of blind obedience and indentured servitude to the System Lords of Orion and the G.O.D. Consortium (Gold and Oil Dynasty).

And these are just a few examples of how self-empowering and all important the study of linguistics is in the world today. How many people are aware that the modern English word *shadow* comes from it's original Egyptian derivation *shetu*? How many people are aware that you can look this up in the Dictionary of Egyptian Heiroglyphics?

In brief, the Shetu were the governing body of free-roaming stone mason masters who held equal influence with the likes of Enlil and Marduk. Eventually, they would overthrow all other system lords and become known as the Shetu Government. We refer to this today as the Shadow Government. The term *shetu* is defined *as those who abduct* and, by having free reign as stone masons in the Old Kingdom, they ended up adopting a second term that is known today as the *Freemason*, henceforth the term 'masonic order'.

I thank my friend Phil Sparks, as well as the mind-blowing shenanigans of Harry Hubbard, Paul Shaffronke and Robert Morning Sky, for setting me straight on the valuable assets and hidden treasures of linguistics. It is now quite clear to me that the only proactive method available for acheiving an educated Democracy and eliminating the religious half-wit degenerates who have taken it from us is to forcibly educate the American population whether they like it or not.

Hey, look at it this way, if it worked for Cuba, it will work for America — unless, of course, you think Cuba is naturally better than the United States.

FOREWORD - 2003

I just finished seeing a very good movie called *The Unsaid* (2001) with Andy Garcia. As the end credits are rolling, I am reminded by the film that I need to get my thoughts down here as there are some things from the first edition that should be *said* now.

You see, over the years there has been time to reflect on what the words in this driven book are actually saying. As time went by, their meanings evolved. As world events unfolded, the defining points of this inspired tome have come to amass a greater sense of clarity and revelation. They will continue doing so as humanity is pushed ever closer to its breaking point and that thin red line between Democracy and the Abduction Phenomenon.

Strangely though, the one golden thread that has remained is of a triumphant testimony to that special friendship with my *confidant*, L. La Mermaid.

I started writing it in autumn of '97 and had it ready for limited edition publication in October of '99. When I had published the first edition, it was with a torrid mix of zeal and trepidation.

Zeal because I had already spent two years writing the damn thing, doing my best to get every last word nailed down with pen and paper so as to accurately capture all social, political and economic aspects of my paranormal excursions into madness. I couldn't wait to launch this first book. By the time it was finished, I felt like the Malcolm X of the Abduction Phenomenon.

Trepidation because what I just wrote in the previous paragraph only explains half of the impetus or motivation that had inspired me to write it in the first place.

You see, at the time, I had a very special person in my life. In many ways, 'L' and her kids have kept a special place in my heart. I do honestly feel that, up to this point at least, the best five years I have had in my life had been with her. Granted, my life has moved on. But there is something of that time with her and the kids that has remained irreplaceable to me.

In that craphole of a year 2000 – the fifth and final year – the shit hit the fan on all levels. It was the worst year for humanity within the Common Era. For America, it was when "president-select" Bush made his Napoleonic coup d'etat and burned the Constitution to pursue a fictional war on behalf of his corporate non-indigenous masters. For me, it was a special friendship going belly up. For reasons that remain regrettable yet understandable, 'L' and I came to a fork in the road and parted ways.

With regard to this book and the issues I have written about, this *confidant* shared many of the same views, perspectives, insights, experiences, knowledge… and feelings. For the purposes of this book, her name remains as L. La Mermaid until such a time when she decides to come out of the closet.

During those years that I knew her, we were taking part in many of the same paranormal revelations, which, at times, included her children as well. For purposes of protecting their identity, they are referred to as the Fantastic Four. The youngest one is named J.M. Starchild and has always held a very special place in my life's journey.

When the book came out, I couldn't wait to show it to 'L' as a surprise. She was the first to see it. *Well… I was dead wrong about that one* and there was a lot of critical bitching and moaning that followed. Her reaction was shocking and unexpected. Yet, as time passed over the years, it became understandable considering the circumstances in that time and place.

It is of that time in 2000 that I wish to draw the reader's attention. You see, when things went to shit, all I could do was watch as both her and the kids were torn out of my life – suddenly and drastically. All I remember from that time is the abyss that I was left in. It would be similar to going into a coma and then beaten with a sledgehammer about fifty-six times.

Upon reflection, I find it interesting that the cusp of two centuries marked the best of times and the worst time in my personal life so far. Oh, and here's a real thrill for all the numerologists and astrologists out there: she disappeared from my life on April 1, 2000.

However, in the time that followed, something quite intriguing had taken place as I was about to get nailed with yet another wake-up call as when I was twenty-one. This time around, I was twenty-nine going onto the big Three-O and feeling like I was at my lowest point in life.

On a whim, I decided to whip out one of my favorite film masterpieces, *The Shawshank Redemption* (1994). I hadn't seen it in a while and felt it would do me some good. [Sidenote: if you compare the original movie poster for the *Shawshank Redemption* to any book illustration of an abduction sequence, you get an identical scenario in both cases. Ex.: Travis Walton]

As I watched the trials and tribulations unfold for Andy Dufresne, Inmate 37927, the movie affected me in a way it never had before. I was Inmate 37927. I was crawling through that tunnel of shit to freedom. As the months passed by, I found myself entering my early thirties reborn. *'What the hell does that mean?'* When I came out on the other side, I was lit up like the fiery Phoenix and transformed into a holy son-of-a-bitch from hell; a relentless, self-empowered truth machine.

Andy Dufresne was just the cherry on the Sundae. Back in the real world, events leading up to this had already been set in motion for ten long years. Go back and read the dedication page and the preface of this book and you'll understand what I am referring to.

On top of that, current important events have arisen, fueling my energies as well. Isabelle and Sophia are two of them. My good friends Eileen and Jim have a little two-year old named Vivian. And of course, there's 'J.M.' She would be seven now. The idea of any of them growing up in this Feudal piss and shit factory we call Democracy leaves me not depressed but rather self-empowered to rage against the machine.

There's the 'quality of life' issue as well, or the lack of it; the struggling, scrapping and hustling that all my friends and family have been going through – and still are. Not one of them has it easy and everyone is within a hair's breath of being out on the street. Unfortunately, I had to realize early in the game that I was born into a karmic circle of poor people who have never witnessed real money. Under our current fascist regime, they never will.

This puts the responsibility on my shoulders entirely to get up off my ass, put away the paintbrushes and pencils and do something that actually alleviates the oppressive migraines of economic slavery within my own karmic circle. No one else in my circle of friends and family can do it at this point as the daily events of everyday life tend to snap your ass into a bear trap of mind-controlling Sisyphian responsibilities.

Now there is always some useless, sickening imbecile who says money can't buy you happiness. *Oh yeah?!?* Hey jackass, neither can poverty. ¡Comprende! Somewhere earlier I had mentioned that liberation and self-empowerment can only come in one main form – linguistics. That one main form is highly important for the mind's eye. Just read Merriam-Webster's Unabridged Collegiate Dictionary. It's the best place to begin. But what about its actual academic applications to your quality of life? Remember, knowledge is nothing without an action to follow up with.

This is where the secondary supporting form of liberation and self-empowerment comes into play – real estate investment. If linguistics paves a road of clarity through an obscure and fabricated past, then real estate investing is the thing that brings it into sharp focus in the present, opening your eyes to the ebb and flow of money in an ancient system of global slavery. You have to know how the rich get to be rich in order to escape poverty.

Don't feel like you are selling out. Your Repto-Sirian masters have been screwing you over for a half-million years. It's time for some payback. Look at it this way: my parents don't have a pot to piss in or a window to throw it from. I can't even do anything for them as I am in the same damn boat. Something has to give and someone has to have the balls to go after it. Aside from that, it may be pathetically romantic to be a poor skanky rat's ass in your teens and twenties. It doesn't say much for you or your parental upbringing but it does ring true. However, if you are still in that same frame of mind in your thirties, then you need to be shot dead on sight.

Lastly, there's that illegitimate silver-spooned dirtbag parading around in the White House. With his obedient Aunt Jemima and Uncle Tom at his side, it seems quite all right with everyone to have the plantation moved from Austin, Texas, to Washington, D.C.

I wonder if Condoleeza Rice and Colin Powell will ever apologize to the American people for their open public endorsement of their own illegal white slavemasters. If they don't, then maybe we should make all the black people go back into the cotton fields of Gehenna. It would be no different if I dropped my pants and mooned all the Jews with a swastika tattooed on my ass. On the other hand, it would probably fit right in with Ariel Sharon's public endorsement of Adolf Hitler's ethnic cleansing policy. If that's not enough to light a fire under *your* ass, then I don't know what is. Need I say more?

*****

I want to say thank you to everyone who did actually take the time to read the book and write a review, letter or in depth essay on it's first run out of the gates. Your time and consideration are most appreciated and have not been wasted or forgotten. The best way I can say thank you is to let you know that some of those articles are now included with the publication of this edition.

If you are ever in trouble or need help, remember to call me. I may be able to aid you in some manner that you never thought possible. I don't have a "bat signal" nor do I wear the letter "S" as an emblem. But I do go by the name UFOteacher… and that is all you will need to find me.

If you are one of those useless shmucks who made an empty promise to me, here's your chance to make up for it – write a review for *this* edition and send it to the publisher!.

INTRODUCTION - 1999

What you are about to read is, hopefully, something that will give each of you a more humane insight into what I have been dealing with since the very beginning. I also hope that most of you will feel much closer to me in the aftermath of such a literary endeavor – maybe even a sense of therapeutic vindication.

Of course, it is unfortunate that some may even despise me as I have stripped myself as naked as possible with an honesty that bears the volatility of absolute truth. This volume, which I have been working on since Fall 1997, is inspired by and comes directly from my work dealing with the Abduction Phenomena, extraterrestrial intervention and all the raging fires in between known as 'an experiment in humanity.'

It is about my relationship with "Mother" – an impassioned matriarch best understood as a bipedal female preying mantis – her swift, diligent and ancient guidance in my life's journey – and the relentless but virtuous veil of protection she extended around me in the form of "downloading" – something that goes well beyond the pale ignorance of my academic, dull–witted detractors.

It is about my calling in life: the artist as one of a multitude called 'teachers of the masses,' avenging sons of the rising Matriarchy, sent to Earth to confront and topple a corrupt, pre-ordained pandemic disease known as the Patriarchy and its dominating control over a genetically, emotionally and psychologically abused human race.

It is about the four horsemen of the Apocalypse, their societal rapists – reptilian overlords and economic slavemasters – and their attempts to hunt down and assassinate all teachers of the masses… and their hybrid children.

It is about the love of a hybrid child, my child; J.M. Starchild, her brothers, sister and their beautiful mother, L. La Mermaid, for whom I would lay down my own life to keep them out of harms way.

Without them there would be no art, no poetry – no reason to live. With them, there is everything – everything I define as being my life. When I look into their mother's eyes, I find the reason to hope, to strive, to live. She has forever changed me – affected my life in ways that I never thought possible.

Lastly, it is about my bonded relationship with my starchild as her guardian and defender for the past four years since she was born, thwarting the efforts of the non-indigenous, soulless assassins of truth – the reptiles of Gehenna.

"Mother" now smiles at me with a sense of accomplishment and great joy that her own earthbound son – her avenging archangel – has evolved this far and embraced his truest purpose and greatest potential in this lifetime.

I know this to be true: the teachers of the masses, artists of the 21st Century, will never allow themselves to be forced to go quietly into the night – never!

As "Mother" once told me years ago: "do not despair –
                                        the one who completes you,
                                        soon she will come…"

Long live the Sisters and Sons of Gaia,
Messengers of the Matriarchy.

Within the heart of the mother and the father
lies the righteous legacy of their daughter.
And so it begins…

"You've really sparked something in my heart…
I know that when I'm with you, the more it feels
like 'something wonderful is going to happen!' "

~ L. La Mermaid
September 9, 1996

"I know you come here a lot because you love me…"

~ J.M. Starchild, age 3
September 9, 1999

Saga:
A Cold Winter

Prelude

Rick Smith

I

A Cold Winter

Please, not another cold winter
emotionally frost bitten
worn to the soul's splinter

Take my trembling hand
let me not wander
from sweetest memories of summers
long and hot
and of Spring's rhythmic thunder
sensual, spiritual

I feel this onslaught to come
Autumn's prancing evil twin
under guise of deceptive 'Fall'
as leaves of Summer past start tumbling

And what of each leaf… a memory
a second, third… fourth
stem over flora spinning torridly
into daunting desolation

The sheen of such leaves mirror
a passion in my heart
as they fall together in unison
I hear them whisper your name

COULD THEY NOT BE SO LOUD?!?

Their whispers clanging together
like Spring's sensual thunder
between our naked bodies

3

a lustful noise, sensual silence
Their mother, the Weeping Willow
of trees,
home to reddest birds, yellowest bees,
comforts me no longer

Her bark grows so cold now –
her hibernation a silent death of my own

I beg not to swallow this coldness,
feel this solitude,
the space from you
as this willow pushes me off
her brittle and weak winter limbs

Please, not another cold winter
this time I will fair not well
for distances too long in travel
too long
as I sink in your wake
to memories left by scents
of your loving spice…my life

The imprint of you left me,
a brilliant angel of pure snow,
one I wish to fall into
before it melts of Winter's twisted yolk

I begin my journey back to you
thoughts of mine, in hope, once again
so I believe in you anew
so to fading leaves I am but a fool

But not before I glance
over clenched and frigid shoulders,
one last bid to farewell – Mother,
her limbs, jagged and torn,
though reborn of Spring,

will hold me no more
No guardian to covet my self
I walk a path muddled, deranged
feeling the scorn of such vacuums,
the loss of what was you,
feeling this chapter a last
as I call to the snow's angel,
hold me with your body's embrace

Reform my weariness,
wash away this onslaught that comes
as I know all too well,
the presence of Spring's thunder,
Summer, moist and hungry,
have gone too afar
with I succumbing to this last
of a cold winter

And what is this?

But one leaf left to dwindle,
to fall just far enough
in my passage ahead

Green in its color, its prime
Awakening!
Mother may yet still hold me

I see it to be sauntering,
gliding on frigid airs
to rest in what I hope for,
imprints of you
in this, a very cold winter

©1997 Rick Smith

5

Rick Smith

II

Journey To The Center

Thoughts of you cross the wind
on whispers crisp and snowy,
leave the taste of fresh desires
thought dead so long ago

And becoming faced with this
I would be the one to grapple
those of many empty fears,
an unbridled nostalgia to what had been

See what you have done,
taken all that I could muster,
turning to molten molasses,
searing the veins beneath one's bark

Crack the egg, the shell, that vacuum,
rescue the one that had existed
as when the Sun shined bright
just like this moment

Invade the vacuum laid before me
before I slip into that hibernation
of emotions turned to ash and soot
prior to this moment

I sink these bleeding, raw knuckles —
'worn to the soul's splinter' —
into pure skin of crystal white…
ease of pain is comfortably numb

A brief respite
only in Winter's moment
as I feel the minions
closing in on delicious kills
and I remember the lessons taught
by all of the one, you Mother

This ancient court of the dance,
a battle of old and new realms,
with the taste of fresh desires
thought dead so long ago.

©1997 Rick Smith

III

My Assassins

She comes to me
upon frigid eves,
Seductress,
candy colored
clown
of my predecessor,
progenitor
of my successor

She spoke
all those things
that lie in
sooted Dusk,
my visions,
the sweat
of my labor

Relentless
was her power,
so too am I,
my Mother's son
to be coaxed,
prodded
by such sweet
ecstasies

Avenging,
taking up her baton,
her shackles,
resisting the one
called Father

The waters of Life,
Sitchin,
Casey,
Nostradamus,
brother

The Baptist Himself

Loving her on Rivers,
birthing the teacher
in Jordan,
in Tigris,
in Euphrates
and Delaware,
the abiogenesis

And to the Father,
nothing,
He who graces
Himself
with my spit

Rick Smith

The mingling stew
of tar,
of bitter vinegars,
giving Him notice
to my
awareness,
my awakenings,
knowing his lies,
deceits,
Capital offense

The realization of my obsession
emanates
in unseen freedoms,
strange bedfellows,
assassins of Truth.

©1998 Rick Smith

IV

Penance

Entering,
fearing his territory,
the tabernacle
of the Father

I absorb
strength,
the remnant
left me
in her body,
vivisected,
lifeless in my arms,
bone white
in her color of ash

Approaching Destiny,
this is what
I was raised for,
doors
of the tabernacle
swinging free,
broken hinges
flayed open
as the walls begin
to sweat their Blood

I lay her
upon altars
where centuries of
bigots,
His centurions,
have been before

11

She gasps,
taking those last steps
where the Dark
meets the Light

Those loud Whispers
come back
in the climax
of her death,
the remaining Blood
of her spayed body
falling
into my palms

I receive the Holy Spirit,
I am her successor

Grinning,
victory seems His,
the Father,
Demon,
man of the Cloth
scowling me

I stand opposed
with feeble attempts
to covet,
protect
the corpse,
once the entity
called Mother.

V

Matriarchy Reborn

Doors
of the Eucharist
lay at the
footsteps
of my Prison

I've kicked them down,
my success
repents the failure
of others

And where is the Superman…

Or could that
have been I,
the Black Sheep of your line

Father,
wavering in stance,
encaged
in stained glass,
encrypted codes,
the Old Order
wells up to face
the bastard son –
the Archangel

This Sword,
it glistens with centuries
of smashed hopes,
my Guillotine,
my Phoenix

13

Its arc,
a vengeance
erupting,
Earth changes
and cataclysms,
all in the name
of Mother

Father's false Prophet,
the agent
of Ancients,
Prince
of my darkness,
He stands
in self-styled mockery,
the ordained One

Clash of Titans,
of pity,
of remorse,
it would come to this
eventually,
Reincarnation's
sick humor

Penetration
of my arc
sinks deep,
deep beneath
the abdomen of
Propaganda,
Evolution
and Ignorance,
scoring
the corruption
of His soul

Exorcism,
my last honor,
cleansing Mother's
Legacy,
His body
a salt lick
of stone,
empty carcass
lying at my feet

Feeling the hand of Fate
pressed upon my shoulder,
her confirmation
of passage –
a loud silence
of new horizons –
succumbs
to chants,
His former Slaves,
"Freedom"
"Freedom"
"Freedom"

The leaf has rooted her ground,
Spring's rhythm
pulsating,
the Mother's Son
reborn…

©1998 Rick Smith

End

Rick Smith

AWAKENINGS

BAIN

Traveled I have,
lightyears
beyond the common,
the average,
the joe

Witnessed have I,
all of it,
tragedies and comedies,
games of chess,
staged plays,
operas
laid out before me

Odysseys,
nightmares,
twenty-five year
mortgages,
it's green grass,
bluest sky,
fading to black

Omens
in the daily
rag,
egotistical,   -
those electronic pompadours

I am laced,
riddled with cancers
misperceived,
viral and
infectious,
as Malcolm
and the Baptist

Digitized anchors
weigh heavy
on the joe –
he watches
in baited breath

He sees new disasters,
manufactured
fabrications
of his dull-witted
awareness

Teachers
falsely slain,
branded antichrists
by entangled webs of
deception,
industrial bi-products
called chaos.

They defeat my common reason.

©1998 Rick Smith

Rick Smith

The Price of Freedom

Immaculate
conceptions
spelling the
abduction
of my innocence

Amber waves
cascading
witnessed truths,
a defilement,
knowledge
becomes agony,
a dissension
in the ranks

I see the night,
tiptoeing
through my bedroom,
laced in carnage,
mayhems
of capitalism,
sins
of my ignorance

Goodbye Hollywood

Heathens,
pseudo intellectuals
shunning truths
in favor of
electric blankets

Commercial
tendencies
shadow their fate.
Homogenized milk,
they lap it
off the bovine's
udder

Salted by the needle,
subtle hints
and odors,
tell tale signs
of rivers tainted,
sheep led to a market

"Hello"
they spoke,
"I am the Media"
they announced
and lastly,
"Give us the Freak"
"Give us the alien"

Yes,
I give my Self to you –
and so,
the slaughter begins…

©1998 Rick Smith

21

Rick Smith

<u>Making It</u>

Angels begin to cry
everytime
a friend succeeds –
I die a little

Materialism,
Imperialism,
Feudalistic
Capitalism
incognito

Agendas,
prophecies,
rolling in poetic
motion,
planes of reality,
checker board
of jaded emeralds

Still they invest
all the while
in such facades,
still they call it
"Making It"

A master facade of masquerades –

And of the angels,
my forebearers,
they began with
a tear,
torrential rains,
foreboding
hurricane,
the world
"making it"
into self immolation,
burned upon
the nightcrawler's stake

Vampires grin with
salivating conquests,
neanderthals howl like werewolves,
minions

Dictators stand atop
that pyramid of chains –
my Global Society

©1998 Rick Smith

The Acerbic S.O.B. That I Am

Roses are red,
violets are blue,
but spaceships are $ilver,
made of $hiny metal too!

This poem is written
for the idiot-buffoon
who thinks green men
are from Mar$ –
and only white men
walk on the Moon!

UFO's are flying $aucers
zipping through the clouds,
like $anta Claus on acid
making whoopy-cushion $ounds!

Happily and merrily
they go about their busine$$,
like lucky charms among the $tars –
do they threaten our existence?!?

The media jumps for joy,
it was just the planet Venu$
or helicopters in the night,
no U.F.O. to meet us :(

It's funny the way Venu$ moves,
up and down,
side to side,
with co$mic $hifts like this
wouldn't our worlds collide Ω

The Human Race – $oooooo $upreme,
with jet engines skirting our sight
DIAGONALLY
– just like that $ilver ray of light Δ

So have no fear,
never mind such threat$,
nor those ridiculous U.F.O.'s
that could never mimic our jet$ ø

All you need to know
are the$e beautiful and wondrous [truth$]
"Little green men are from Mar$ –
And white men ONLY
are allowed on the Moon."
<|-(THE<(0)>END)-|>

©1998 Rick Smith

<u>Traitor</u>

Inconspicuous
to shortsighted drones,
suitable for mass consumption

Visible,
usual scapegoat,
served on public display,
how convenient

(ray of light piercing prison walls)

Outcast,
the one who slept
with a cosmic
mystery,
non-indigent lover

(I live to tell of it)

An epiphany,
gravedigger of public interest,
walking on fires,
universal
conviction,
coffins nailed shut,
as Snow White
feeds me
from the tree
of lost knowledge

Her venom –
    the forbidden
    of archaeology

The traitor among liars

<u>Cleopatra</u>

I saw you,
standing by seas
called Life,
figment of imaginations
groping,
hoping your beauty
a reality

I fell towards love...
...you faded to sands of time

I died more than a little,
my soul watched
as you turned away,
silhouetted princess,
hot and glistening
in vapors of a star

Pieces torn of me,
the most important parts –
Do you think of me?

And here we approach
that sultry eve of Summer,
an end to a past,
new cycles,
with musty thoughts
clung to passionate desires,
longing the Great Return

Do you think any less of me?

You,
whom I see every time
on wisps of wind,
scents on air,
sounds in song

Yes,
I think of you
many nights over...
...and mornings...
just as the Sun kisses my body

Do you miss my touch?
- emotional,
- physical,
- spiritual,
- myself... I do

I want this reality,
to immerse myself in it...
...in my heart where you are real

In my heart...
YOU ARE THE ONE I FEEL

As dawn concludes
another empty evening,
my mind trails through
alternate dimensions,
nights spent with you,
filling our hungers,
sharing thoughts… bodies,
heated rhythms

Love in slow motion

So where can you be?

Golden Aphrodite,
I miss the Cleopatra
as I hear awakenings
in my hot summer nights

~ to L. La Mermaid, with love
©1999 Rick Smith

<u>Revival</u>

Stepsister of wicked winds
from urban North,
rural South,
the Slut that laid
with wretched devils,
setting brother against brother,
sister against mother,
father against nations

I know the face
of your maker,
the vigilant patriarch,
false God rotting
in the stains
of my enslaved corpse

Out of the desert
I come,
a drop of paint
sliding
down a blank canvas,
tumbleweeds
of light and shadow –
they give me form

Blistering Sun,
it burns a spectrum,
Gnosis,
into my being —
I am fully exorcised,
metamorphosized,
revived,
a genetic wildcard
- Thoth
- Zeus
- Christ
- Buddha

Jokers of a silenced
knowledge,
dormant minotaurs,
I, caged,
the maddened bull,
have been awakened

And So It Begins...

Trenches of my past,
these tears,
they burn
deep into my flesh,
face of my genes

Nostalgia,
sublime depression,
a sense of loss,
days gone by
that could not be kept
to present pace

The future,
my oyster,
lays tracks
across my grave,
a residual effect,
emotions lying in dust

(a friend's aging photograph : cancer's latest
victory)

(a lover's letters smothered in vacancies :
once heated passions)

Loved ones,
the baby brother,
engaged… married

Mother, I was not prepared for this

Days gone by,
I am betrayed
in the present,
my mind,
lost in vacuums
of a past

Blissful times,
fresh,
young,
when last I kissed her,
that lover
in the letters.
Manuscripts of happiness

And then…
first calling,
first amendment to my being,
by entities maternal,
extraterrestrial

Warned was I...
such treasures never last,
falling to my knees

Six years,
eons... ages ago,
all has happened
in split seconds
of a sadist,
Father Time

(whiplash : nostalgia : backwash : deja' vu)

He remains an aftertaste
in the continuum
of my time,
my space,
trench warfare
in the DNA of my race

©1999 Rick Smith

THE CALLING

Rick Smith

<u>Baptism</u>

With sweaty palms
moist
in the blood
of ancestors,
come to me –
I await

Your origins,
such high plateaus,
awaken
the sleeper,
Cidonia's
hibernation

Release the Kracken,
it's tree
of knowledge,
my Cabala,
lying just beneath
sacred tombstones,
my Sphinx

Masonic builders
of propaganda,
they run from
your sight,
that cruel line
of vision,
a grueling truth.

They mock me,
flies
locked in
hermetically sealed
homogenies

The pact,
your visitation,
our conjugal bliss,
I know this all
as I know you,
foreign lover,
non-indigent,
illegal and
hunted to extinction

Your fever of fire,
virus
in my veins,
quenched
with sweaty palms,
moist
in your blood
of lines,
my baptism

©1998 Rick Smith

Rick Smith

<u>Communion</u>

The art,
not you,
keeps me warm
in solstices,
equinoxes

Pulling
her canvas linens
around my skin,
she makes love,
symbiosis,
to me

I,
the mere moth
entombed
among catacombs,
predecessors.
Her painted resin
fills my pores,
feasting my
metamorphosis,
feeding off me

To the flame
I plunge,
seared,
forged are we,
her scorn and mine –
Phoenix and Mantis,
mating eagles to doves

I am awakened,
the first of many
to come...
...channeled...

...downloaded,
conjugal terrains

In her relentlessness
she is
gorgeous,
her torment –
my delicious exotica

In her worst
state,
a perfection
in altered seduction.
Upon twilight's end,
blazing chariots descend,
toppling
the remains
of fifty-hour days

Rick Smith

"Play with me",
words sent
into the void,
a love letter
straight from her heart,
piercing fringes
of Mother's Earth

"Be mine –
for I am yours",
And I hers.
Between
stretched canvas
and
sordid bedsheet
lies the imprint,
scent of her mark

<u>Confirmation</u>

I am –
caged in iron
masks,
Cain's Abel,
while all the days
lost and won
to Napoleons,
Caesars,
prostitutes of Yaldobaoth

I am –
honesty,
humanity's birthright,
the fool
who employed
Lucifer…
emperor with no clothes,
possessing all the wool
stripped
atop sheep's hide,
a societal slumber

43

Rick Smith

I am –
teacher… creator,
weapon of the Unbegotten,
silent and deadly,
blacklisted
by all the days
lost and won
to Heir Hitlers,
their Anunnaki,
and four horsemen
seen racing chariots of gods
like misbegotten warlords

<u>Boxing With The Past</u>

Obscurity,
side blinder's
weapon,
guiding my hand,
my spirit,
beyond monuments
of silvery moons
and bitter continents

Blood on my hands
…paint,
reflections
of a god
…canvas.
It wears a face –
Mars,
as I am doomed
to perfection

Standing steadfast,
I lean against
icy winds,
waves,
fleets of vengeance
hunting sons,
daughters –
its foreign ancestry

Forsaking the teacher,
meager,
feeble,
an idiot of amusement,
they never see
the master
of plans,
its ruse
just behind my eyes

Taken under wing,
obscurity,
once my enemy,
becomes allied,
my salvation,
it's army of
Trojans –
strategic ballets

Fleets of vengeance
unwittingly march
upon blooming
mine fields,
new ages of
enlightenment,
eroding Mars,
thawing Antarctica,
their maker revealed

©1998 Rick Smith

<u>Holy Spirit</u>

Double helix,
enflamed DNA,
a chromosomal orgy
in the quickening
of my generation

Gnosis,
rage of freedom,
the teacher of masses,
metalinks
of humanity's birthright,
in excommunication
from corporate bloodlines,
molested hatchlings
of an antichrist

Kill the mudslinger...
propagandist spin doctor
of old lies

Protect the messenger
of my phoenix,
livid spirit,
an eruption,
Joan of Arc
reincarnated
from warm graves,
molten catacombs
of Mother's magma,
sign of times
past and present

Listen to her calls
    - Vesuvius
    - St. Helens
    - Great El Nino

Listen to the Devil,
bastard in the details
or my dormant
habitual genes

©1998 Rick Smith

Future Shock

A little girl,
the One you see
in urban alleys,
suburban sumps,
the knotted trash,
dirt smear across her eyes,
teacher of the masses
withering in denial

This little boy,
he sees Death,
a societal train wreck
rising from the street,
a grin across its jaws,
masked visage,
the face of Cidonia,
rotting cesspool
of a broken Paradise

Our little girl,
vagabond in the making,
an "X" burned into her head,
foresight of a third eye,
she knows
this ancient menace,
its intent to kill,
to succeed

That little boy,
a state of desperation,
resisting Death's grasp,
temptations
laid before him...
- drug dealer
- pimp
- gangsta
- hustler
- King Herod

Your little girl,
holding fast
to a humanity
betraying her faith,
ravaging his soul,
their raging spirit,
as we the people
look the other way,
denying his existence,
her identity,
teacher of the masses,
Mercury's messengers
withering
in our ignorance,
selective genocide
of our social denial

©1999 Rick Smith

The Last Laugh

Retribution is hers,
it lies with
avenging sons – creators,
the Matriarchy,
suburban phoenix,
red cells radiant
among pools,
incestuous blood,
arisen
from ashen sumps,
squalid vacuums,
repository
of interdimensional
wastelands,
quantum leaps
in spiritual decay

Invaded territories
of her Self,
a power hungry prince
        - christian fundamentalism,
war cries bellowed
from the darkside of moons –
        "Honor Thy Father..."
        "Honor Thy Master..."

Oh yes,
the Thing that killed her!

©1998 Rick Smith

<u>Nightmoves</u>

Nightmoves…
- an abduction
- first contact
- paranormal pestilence

A movement
in the dance of life,
a repose in the
dusk of dawn…
- a meteor
- one comet
- memories shot amidst crystal twilight

A moment to breathe
among pawns of war,
Adamus faces Adapa,
teachers confront assassins

Humanity combats its own state of alienation

…night moves

<u>My Sensuality</u>

Pulsating thoughts spanning a time,
waiting for hungers that are quenched,
and then to my eyes
you appear –
I, in scorched sunshine,
am drenched

My search in subconscious
comes to a fore
raining on my soul,
I now breath

Once I knew you
when I was more whole,
as you walk in the light
my spirit seethes

I run to you… obsession,
must kiss you
        - hold you
            - make love…
Need your touch as I remember
…revelation,
my ultraviolet dove

Mother,
to you is my allegiance
and know it is you
I defend –
but I must,
with her,
share what is mine,
be swallowed whole
by feline enchantress,
bonded to her

53

Rick Smith

desperate fever
of wholistic steamy
reverence

Take witness,
look to this soul's companion,
protect the half of me
more worthy
than the half you chose

Gaia,
I adore you in nature
but she remains
my lover,
my saviour,
freedom unhinged

Escaping,
I go the paths she leads,
wallowing in sexual tints,
her passionate tones,
scent of fragrant mints

No longer just a man –
with her
I am human,
      - shades of every man
      - every woman
enlightenment
in upheaval,
in this time,
my life… my sensuality

~ to L. La Mermaid, my "confidant"
©1998 Rick Smith

L. La Mermaid

Everytime...
it happens
as she walks
amïdst the feast
of my emotions

Faster...
the speed
of my pulse,
a climax of lust,
a seasoning for love

To touch her
just once...
and I surrender
in her arms,
her lips,
embracing skin,
a body of soul

Softness of her kiss,
passage to Eden,
a heated paradise
of sensual havoc,
locked among
legs and thighs,
fulfillment,
her smile gracing
my being

Wishing upon her,
as stars fade to dawn,
and the anguish
commences,
shattered dreams,
wanton desires,
the hunger of ages

(No…)

I awake
to emptiness,
inescapable,
hollowed
to an empty shell

(Come back…)

Gone –
as hints of devastation
seep into me…
…the ring…
…she is married…
            …unhappily married

Our paths cross,
she smiles,
recognition
of night's splendor,
cosmic
interludes,
Dali's dreamscape,
passionate collision
upon paranormal terrain

We are alone,
finally,
together
in fleeting moments,
at last,
solitude becomes Heaven,
I speak my mind…
     …thoughts and feelings…
         …her smile remains

(I want you… I need you)

Everytime…
as she walks beside me,
in love with me
in love with her
in defiance of manicans,
corpses,
floating sewer rats –
    - her father
    - her husband

My mind – I see her,
my heart – I feel her,
upon my self I know her,
longing for
my sister of the night

Liberation at last…
my life for you

~ for you, my "sister," with love
©1998 Rick Smith

Rick Smith

THE HORSEMEN COMETH

Rick Smith

<u>Xenophobic</u>

Death,
in the family,
in the field
of dreams,
a forbidden planet,
poisoned
fruits of labor,
its conquests –
devoid of virtue,
the economics of slavery

Stricken to the core,
so deep,
riddled with strategies,
your agendas filling
Mother's breast
with snapped bones,
skeletons
of her children

Paranoiac agonies flex
in your pronounced
squelches,
my polluted offspring

How natural
your grin
upon the infant's
chain addiction

X-Factor,
generation of generations,
fallen prey
to malignant prodigies,
genetic distortions,
your protegés,
your celebration,
talons of the
global oppression

Opportunities
lay a heap
upon burning gateways,
unfettered passage
for armies of darkness,
your path a guarantee –
the suburban dream,
a living demon,
betrays
Democracy
at last

Proprietors invasion,
such evasive
maneuvers,
minions disrobe!
- battalions
- conglomerates
- monopolies

The gridlock of Marshall Law

Rick Smith

Your vacuums,
prisons of society,
chain not my vision,
not my spirit,
not me

I see it approaching,
our distance
swiftly nearing

First of Four,
you dismantle my humanity.
May you not know,
as we lock in lines of sight,
what lies,
in ash and cinder,
beneath my skin –
poetic justice

Pulsating,
throbbing,
relentless eruptions,
I release the Kracken,
lover's mark,
Mother's scorn,
Phoenix rising –
that moist blood
adorning swords,
forging my helix
upon hot coals

It is the edge of all midnight
which harbors a split
in the vacuum of space.

©1998 Rick Smith

<u>Sexism</u>

Red Meat,
pieces
dangling from
sharpened teeth

Sinking
gutted jaws
into table scraps,
leftovers
of chauvinism

The Ax,
it's grinding wheel
reaching
a halted release,
bald to the core –
her existence,
her one
sustaining
factor...

Jealously,
vendetta
against the Mother,
maiden bitch
of slain eyes

Fingers of blame,
Scorn's
poignant rebuttal,
pointed towards
Island Ellis

Shells of hatred,
Walls –
harbingers of deceit,
coating her every
bare
attribute
in paper thin diamonds

Washingtons,
Lincolns,
U.S. Grants –
glazing
spayed nipples,
stitched vaginas,
clay molds
and burnished curves
of naked commercialism

Lab rat
to Patriarch's invasion,
her initiation,
a final
blow
among her destined
jobs

Bitter Daughter,
manifestation
of Liberty's
whore,
assassin of
founders –
of homogenized truths

Upon breadbaskets
of world hunger,
Xenophobic solos
present duets
in deadly arias

Eye to eye,
greeting her
bloodened lips,
the only one to do so,
and so the dance
begins

One
is now Two,
conniving Spawn,
vengeful Slut,
Frankenstein's mate awakened

©1998 Rick Smith

Rick Smith

<u>Racism</u>

I was free,
I am you
and you…
me

Remember the whip,
force
or your will,
cutting deep
beneath the strength
of my back,
scars left me,
heiroglyphs,
historical memoirs,
bitter sweet genetics

Reincarnation,
my brother's keeper,
prodding,
pushing me
as I become
the better,
the stronger,
the faster
one

Minister of thugs,
pushing
the Nationalist's drug,
I see the face
of your nemesis,

reflections
of you,
poisons
in communal schools,
segregation

Extraterrestrial slavemaster,
cracking God's whip,
feeding us tainted lots,
lies and anecdotes,
annals of Genesis,
like serpents
in the grass
of suburbia's front lawn

I see you dance
through gardens
of good
and of evil,
drowning our miseries
among underground cesspools,
charcoaled aromas
and my neighbor –
    his vacuum sealed ghetto

Dressed in white,
a concealed deception,
swinging the blooded
reaper,
you join two
and become three…
    - Spawn
    - Slut
    - Stigma

©1998 Rick Smith

Nationalist: into the void

Viking,
astronaut,
you misguided fool,
a highly revered
crash test
dummy

Blonde supremacy,
a trophy
given you,
baited
with billowed
veils—
red meat,
white milk,
blue skies
blinding the eyes

You become unveiled
in armed conflict,
a self-perpetuating
theme song
bent along
Confederate delinquency,
legacies of General Lee

Cotton bathed
henchmen
saluting
a moth infested
rag,
saturation point
of blood
milk
and sky

Clandestine thoughts
of the terrorist,
Palestine's
liberation,
fertile crescents
looted,
reptilian
ancestors
in the grassy knoll

Squads of facades
spew forth,
their mechanisms –
the big lie,
a high
we dare not
come off

Teachers,
seers,
the beckoning
of one
to esoteric codes,
food of the gods,
left rancid
by fraternal twins of the intellect
        - Arrogance (Enki),
        - Chauvinism (Enlil)

Deities
of dominion
meet
in mine shafts
of the soul,
dancing
in quartets,
cavalcades
of hooded equestrians,

four of four,
marching
to bandwidths of silence,
shredding all
that is the spirit,
societal collapse,
my personal desolation

Mother,
a witness
to this rape,
sheds her skin,
lashing at
a bastard race
   - you
   - me
   - the next door neighbor

our vacuum sealed ghettos

De-evolved chimps
moaning like gutted cattle,
barbarians at the gate,
while four
merge
to one,
social unification,
genetic assimilation,
facile domi-nation...

the Stigma,
the Spawn,
the Swastika
and his Slut

©1998 Rick Smith

<u>Abortion</u>

Her innocence,
lying face down
in the gutter,
pummeled,
assaulted

It drowns somewhere
in the Ganges,
invasions
of her naive
ignorance,
the Maiden's
last voyage

Swelling,
her agony becomes
a squalor
in withering
flames,
raining down
a smoldering torch

Confrontations,
the monkey
on her back,
as the oldest
of orders
combats the newest
of ages

Her children,
zombies and footsoldiers,
divided by
oceans of intolerance

The brittle
and gray,
sins of the Father,
selective
in their ignorance,
dividing the masses

The freshness
of youth,
correcting such sins,
forging
promised lands,
unacceptable realms

Her progeny,
two lands,
divided over
mental rapes of humanity,
unforgivable truths

The chopping block,
she remembers it well,
a resting place
for Herod's head

A decision to be made
with no point
of return

In the end,
it's her body
face down
in Hudson,
in Delaware,
with illegitimate
offspring –
racist
sexist
nationalist
xenophobic

The meek inherit
lands
littered by graves,
scarecrows of
the Illuminati

My Accusers

Metaphysician,
always the one,
locking me in
the vacuum sealed
mentality

Armchair intellectual,
always the one –
      uneducated,
telling tales,
propaganda,
how I never
existed

Zealot,
fundamental
to a core,
labeling
my kind
messengers
of a demon –
      God of zealots

(I smile with pride)

Strike me down –
      I become more...
      more than you imagine

Touch me –
      human...
      more than you

Love me –
    everlasting…
    longer than perceived

Curse me –
    gift of gnosis…
    that which stings
    in Twilight's dawn

Talk to me –
    wisdom…
    that which is absurd

Profanity of pre-historic ancients

Casted to depths
of a double
standard,
speculations of faith
    - giant squid
    - black holes

While Atlantis,
evident
to a fault,
burns at the stake

Assault
of accusations,
astronomers with rags
soaked
in vinegar –
    saturation
    of my wounds

To my right,
Sitchin… godfather,
my left,
Sagan… laughingstock,
in front,
a sea of riots

All investments,
remains of a day,
lost
in Hister's big lie

Moral
absolutism
forged
in Ezekiel's vision,
Sumerians rejoice…

…VINDICATION

Saganites wimper
in suicidal
tendencies,
pitfalls of science,
propaganda
of logic

And I…
(smiling with pride)
…I marvel
at liberations of truth,
genocide
of my accusers

Everyone dies,
but not everyone truly lives

Rage Of Silent Truths

Hallelujah,
paranoia,
I have seen the holy ghost

Spirit in the sky
cemented to shadows
of rock
- Sodom
- Gamorrah
- Nagasaki
- Hiroshima
- Arabia
- America

Strata in the veins of revenge...

Dance of demons,
inhumane winter,
condemning the promise
of humanity
in sands of time
fused
to heated tendencies
of ash and soot,
boils and stys...

...cysts of the womb,

genetic titans
rigging the abortion
of Eridu's Valhalla,
Tiamat's Kingdom Come,
Earth's Mother

Rick Smith

How nice...

to throw in the towel,
join the cattle,
chorale of sheep,
silence of the lambs

How pleasant...

to drown in happiness
fostered
by serpents,
dogs
of molested stars,
afterburn
of a system lord,
birth of Suburbia

It is a paradox
in life sentences,
an economic slave
revisiting Genesis
in this,
our newest century

The Back Left Corner
Of Heaven

Stabbed
through the back,
as Life's elixir
runs cold
upon my body,
crimson tide

The blade,
a glistening ore
alloyed to my blood.
I witness my life,
reflections
  - was
  - is
  - could have been…

My lover,
my child,
calling to me
from higher realms,
how long I have waited

Friends and family,
comrades in arms,
beckoning my presence,
reunite in greener pastures,
how much I have yearned

Angel of Death,
she comes to me,
my emancipation,
I am relinquished,
I am free to go

...gleaming from a double-edged sword

My nemesis,
grinning,
malevolent,
unaware...

Scaled relic,
mid-eastern neanderthal,
mid-western derelict,
worshipping the finger of his
DOG : GOD
    - gold-plated uzi
    - greased pestilence
    - territorial country

The Father,
spiked fingers,
crest bone and all,
always a sight to see
through eyes
of high society

©1999 Rick Smith

INTO THE FRINGE

– finale –

Rick Smith

Dogs Of War

Illegitimate
children,
they command
the ranks

Droves of
clones,
men
in pitch black
of Night's
shadow,
forsaken
agents
of the Pandemic,
a state of
affairs
driven
into the ground

Blood stained soil
neatly padded down,
paved roads
of Suburbia,
with fatal
conclusions
carved into blacktop,
Night
marking its territory

Your children,
our legacy
futuristic waves
chained
to unnatural ecstasy,
grayer pitches of ice,
frozen tidal wave –
the stagnated swamp
of used needles... wet condoms

Their clean-up crew,
Federal
Emergency
Management,
in stark white,
Damage Control,
reinforced
chain links
of logical ignorance,
a formula for addiction

The breaking point
approaches,
Men in White
unmasked,
Men in Black
revealed
and the Dogs of War
drool
over a convenience
in their invasion

Our instant gratification
justifies the means –
Humanity's liquidation

Silence Of The Lambs

Running,
sheep to a slaughter,
their desperation
swells
to a lather,
gratification,
sensory deprivation

My daughter to be,
her son to come,
a nail in the coffin
for new generations

I pound
my fist
against the cage,
zoological zombies,
aimless nomads,
disciplined tribes,
- intranets
- sitcoms
- soap operas

Monsters of the Id,
the dance of life
unfolding
just beneath
manufactured thoughts,
couch potatoes
of electronic media

©1998 Rick Smith

Rick Smith

<u>Neighbors</u>

And they're OFF!

All the lonely people –
I know from where
they come,
the rant
of consumer reports:
    "Don't be LATE!
    Act NOW!
    Supplies are running OUT!"

As if to encapsulate
humanity's spirit…
    - a bottle of bleach,
    - a flask of steak sauce

Ingredients called lies in Dolphin Safe Tuna

Racing,
their desperate struggle,
acquiring
material superiority,
breakdown in the making,
commodities run dry,
a dividend
in the vacuum of one's soul

I leave
my Levit shelter,
the white picket fence,
sitting beside
a derelict neighbor…
…together
we watch the Addams
eating the Cleavers alive,
modern day Helter Skelter

"He's mad", they whisper,
looking my way,
or is it the one
living
in corrugated boxing?
(shelter of nomadic hordes)

"You brought this upon us",
this is what they shout
looking OUR way –
        the gypsy is slayed,
        I, stoned,
        back into Dark Ages
        my suburban shelter

Therein lies
a clash of cultures,
extraterrestrial
friends and foes,
intervention
in the banter
of caged souls,
a dialogue in the void…

"Insane"	: to your convenience
"Evil"	: to your ignorance
"Antichrist"	: to your existence
"What are you?!?"	: your worst nightmare
"Who are you?!?"	: your next door neighbor
"Bow down"	: head like a hole
"before the one"	: black as your soul
"you serve"	: I'd rather die
"you're gonna get"	: than give you control

"what you deserve"

I,
the grain of sand
on shores of millions,
this,
the masquerade of angels

©1998 Rick Smith

<u>Going to War</u>

Shores of Babylon,
my tour,
this duty,
legions
of rose tinted
thorns

I kiss the rain,
a dripping agony
from maiden's
eyes,
I am prepared,
in love,
I do not
turn
that other cheek

This time – to the end

Refusal
to bend amidst
winds of war,
the rank
stench
of urban snakes,
rural moles

I walk
among them all,
property damage,
state
of existence,
vacancies
in the soul
of intellectual sloths

Their masters,
termites,
marching upon
Washington,
the underground vortex,
forbidden passage
among spools
of power,
domination,
sanctioned embargoes
on one's humanity

Golden Fleece,
they loom
in the sky,
messengers
of Mother,
Mercury's battalion

Spinning zephyrs,
they light my path
in uphill battles,
technological tumors,
patriarchal
debauchery,
poetic endings
to my age of innocence

Mentors,
peers,
successors,
united...
    - my brother's keeper
    - my sister's son,
linked in time,
in space,
my mind

A chain,
strong
to the weakest,
and I...
    ...I am not so weak this day

©1998 Rick Smith

<u>Confrontation</u>

I saw you come back,
childhood demon,
my father,
manifestations of long ago,
sending a blow
to your daughter,
my "confidant"

Flickering light,
combustionible flame,
wellspring of cauldrons
arise
within my spirit

Rings of fire
ignite the Phoenix,
I surround your lair

A mother's education,
grace of a mantis,
fury of divine lives
coming to the surface
upon my being

I tear you down
on your knees,
a smile
smacking into my face

Today,
a good day to die,
to live,
to die again,
as rivers of ignorance,
baited,
climax
in a screeching halt

They gawk at me
(no surprise)
in utter astonishment,
as I deliver him
a final blow

Love letters,
wholistic obsession,
written in smoke
and burning lust –

"Thou shalt not touch the mother,
thou shalt not touch the daughter,
my sister,
my lover,
those whom dreams
fall upon
in heated eves
of Twilight"

My serpentine
menace,
slipping out of grasp,
you fall,
like slugs eating maggots,
salt licks
of Gamorrah,
tar pits of reflection,
soul's dysfunction
in your former self

93

Take heed,
Conspirators' Hierarchy,
this omen
of cosmic
proportion,
I the exorcist,
the mother's son,
my sister's brother

Leave in peace
dear Lords,
economic clans
of Araman,
my spirit soars
against your tide,
I stand witness
to misbegotten children,
corporate titans,
powers of addiction
spewed…
   …from the horns of a poisoned heifer

~ to L. La Mermaid,
I will always be there… always

©1998 Rick Smith

<u>Genetic Legacy</u>

They are coming,
so am I,
thorns of plenty
combating
English Ivy,
empire of his sun

Has he no shame,
no understanding,
of her forest,
burial grounds
of dancing bones,
the Mantis,
her seeds laid
in lush pastures

Branches and limbs
extend to the twigs,
budding the blossom,
birth of my calling

The leafing begins,
she sheds her
children,
we descend
upon suburban sod,
a cancer of unkempt weeds

Her allies,
our cousins
distant
upon Jesse Trees,
my genealogy,
they await the beckoning,
starborne healers
of biological evolution,
global revolution

<u>Crossing Over</u>

Ecumenical sermons,
jigsaw puzzles in time,
I heave
such biblical legacies,
shattering the window
to all worlds

Ascent,
humanity's promised land,
logos of spirit,
atoms dance
on the fingertips
of gnosis,
the brush
and the quill

Descent,
of galactic communities,
archetypes,
angels and demons,
they come to life
in biomorphic realities,
transdimensional gods
begin
initiations of Earth

Judas and his priests,
playwrights
of the demon,
freely raze
an ecosystem,
global quarantines

Rick Smith

Preludes
of awareness,
rites of passage
through
Akashic records,
global consciousness,
convergence
of past with present
upon future fates,
written
in bloodlines
called
extraterrestrial

Judaic cabals,
coursing through rivers
   - Christian
   - Muslim,
stand steadfast
in quests of tyranny,
checkmates
in the ley lines
of chess,
chaos in world orders,
futile attempts
scuttling
new ages of enlightenment

Revolution,
chickens coming home
to roost,
as we wash away
soiled blood,
humanity eclipsed
in a pale moon light

©1998 Rick Smith

Endgame

Army of the Dog
and his Comodo Dragons,
devouring the apple
of my pie,
surrounding perimeters,
gutting the seas,
final assaults
in back alleys
of human desolation

Hand of comfort
on my shoulder,
I hear the whispers
upon
winds of war,
echoes of my former youth –

    "Remember
    my son,
    I do this for you,
    for the many,
    for one and all…
    remember,
    you are the successor,
    my lasting hope"

Helical elements
homing in,
slamming shut
upon her,
a descent
into abyssal chasms,
coal mines of slavery,
cotton fields
called Gehenna

The place of conspirators
and well laid plans
attempting
to rape my spirit,
a gift
of the Mother,
target site of ignorance

Breath of life,
her splintered hints,
they come through
in deafening clarity,
as the Earth
splits
to core firmaments...

...I AM FREED

Legions of Light
isolated no more,
the universe,
Elders,
holding their breath,
the Kracken readies,
mounting
crests of Everest,
rooftops
of the world,
delivering
the gift of gnosis,
skeletons
in the closet

Nazi drones,
legacies of appeasement,
scrambled,
panic stricken,
in poetic deaths
to twenty-five year
mortgages

Stockade fences catch afire,
I watch
Ignorance burn
with its whore,
Suburbia,
to gutters
of annihilation

Rick Smith

Smoke billows
to red skies bled dry
by institutional thought,
slayed
upon Pilgrim's Rock

Slavemasters withdraw
to bitter asylum,
camouflage of black heavens,
Nebiru,
huddled
in paranoiac sorrow,
so it is written,
so it is done,
let the games begin

Amid all ash and soot
lies the logos,
mythic blue whales,
and her sisters
    - the forest
    - willows,
whispering in triumph
upon
silent victories…

…RESURRECTION
of the man in the Moon!

©1998 Rick Smith

My Starchild, My Daughter (a message)

Hope
of my tomorrow
lays in fresh young palms,
your small fragile hands

You...
the spark,
a flame,
ignited from passions
genuine,
real,
your mother and I

Between the sheets
of mated lovers,
within twilight's night,
a paranormal calling
met our wanton desires

Starchild,
glow of our life,
you and your siblings,
seedlings
of the interstellar

Synchronicity,
first time
meeting your mother,
nine months
carrying you

Then –
you were born!

We simply knew...

...you belonged to us

With a promise
of new beginnings
in the continuum of time,
of our space

The best of moments,
so inspiring,
wonderful in my life,
come from you

Days to remember –
    - one year old... the message I wrote you
    - two years old... holding you close
    - three years old... teaching me chess
    (in your own way)

Wishing to tell
your beautiful mother,
I have looked into her eyes,
found my soulmate,
the reason to live

My life,
to live it with her,
with you,
your sister,
your brothers,
a bliss I truly desire

The message
I left for you,
in sealed memories
of a newborn's
first year,
to find me
as I hope you still
remember me,
my face,
my name

Gifted daughter of cosmic wombs,
will you remember me, know my face?

I wish to tell you
all that I know,
watch you grow –
     - student to mentor
     - child to adult…

To pass on all that I am,
the artist,
the teacher,
to you

Might you paint
a masterpiece,
strum an instrument,
write a poem
for your generation,
I would want to stand witness,
as you evolve
from starchild
to teacher of the masses

(like daughter : like father : like daughter)

Gifted one,
we will always nurture you,
protect you,
defend you,
even in your darkest hour –

As we always have

You…
coming of age,
our truest purpose,
to let you know…
        …forever have we been there
        …forever have we loved you

Forever have I loved your mother

©1999 Rick Smith
~ to J.M. Starchild, January 8, 2017,
with all my love,

and L. La Mermaid,
within all my hopes and dreams,
within all my strongest passions,
there you are… you and the kids, always
I love you

con todo mi amor
te quiero,
love Rick

End

EPILOGUE
"Into The Roots"

Rick Smith

Within a night,
where it had begun,
I returned,
academia
of my former Self,
my home
of engrossed concealments

Energies were thrust,
a moment
of triumph,
victory dance,
end of an era,
May 1998

Fellow compatriots,
mentors,
former peers,
savoring
the fall
of pre-historic bureaucrats,
interred legacies

Emotional memoirs,
nostalgic blitzkrieg,
my calm exterior
besieged within

And there she stood... in the rain

Wet droplets
glistening
off raven eyes,
rainbows in obsidian,
hypnotic,
skin of naples yellow
adorned in draperies
of evening mist

Mantis
of guardian angels,
greeting her
in kisses of baptism,
we stood in silence,
festivities absorbed,
laughter of my friends

With roots
ancient as soil,
she felt my weakness
in despair,
loss and remembrance,
dislocated
from my birthing

Coursing through my being,
I felt her roots,
tribal burial grounds,
into my mind,
around my heart –
    she spoke to me

"Forgotten
have you
that which started
with you?"

My beginnings here,
conversations
with her,
passions flourishing
into unearthly callings,
yes… I remember well

"See
do you not
all the impressions
of you?"

My former mates,
friends with a common foe,
their success,
fueled
to make a difference,
their powers of
creation = exploration
exploration = utilization
utilization = revelation
revelation = creation
an affirmation
of my inspiration

"A role
in their present
your past does play."

The vacuum
of my Self,
no longer so apparent,
gave out
to watersheds,
renewed understanding,
sharpness of clarity

Before us
stood a future,
possibilities abounding,
positive angst
of youth... my friends,
    - the good
    - the bad
    - the best

I join them,
the truest
of human beings,
with the kiss
of confirmation,
as she leaves
between the raindrops

Bouncing off the mist,
her seeds echoing in me –

"Bite the bullet
then spit it back,
the end of all eras,
a death to all antichrists,
will come
in the forge
of new tomorrows,
a daughter... your child."

And all her leaves...
    ...they fell to the ground.

<u>AFTERWORD</u>

From The Desk Of...

Rick Smith

byron lebeau

A Letter To The Author

November 19, 1999

Dearest Rick,

Thanks for baring your soul in your magnificent *Legions of Light* presentation: I love you unconditionally as my true friend and co-worker for the Truth.

There are so many emotions touched upon – executed with piercing pathos – that I, lebeau, can scarcely decide how or where to begin. Let me just say that both *The Back Left Corner of Heaven* as well as *Genetic Legacy* left a superior effect on my soul/spirit... *Xenophobic* was also an extraordinary expression of your poetic use of words.

I was touched by your candidness and believe I have intuited the situation. I have felt the pain of not being able to completely harness that of whom I loved – and it caused me much, much pain... whatever... true growth comes with much pain.

As busy as I am and distracted by some serious stuff, I made it a point to read the whole book. WOW! You set the scene in fine fashion in the last stanza of *Journey To The Center:* // a battle of old and new realms // with the taste of fresh desires // thought dead so long ago.

I like the way you expressed the feeling to the "Father" in *My Assassins:* // He who graces // Himself // with my spit // The realization of my obsession // emanates // in unseen freedoms, //

And in *Making It:* Angels begin to cry // everytime // a friend succeeds - // I die a little // } Apt expression for the Kingdom of Man.

In *Revival* I loved the depiction of the Vigilante Patriarch: // false God rotting // in the stains // of my enslaved corpse // } Boy - are you ripe for going from death to the Kingdom of Man to the true beauty of the

115

Rick Smith

Kingdom of God! Excellent. This process is keenly manifested in the Gospel of Thomas!

In *THE CALLING* section, I loved both *Communion* and *Confirmation:* by describing yourself as // the mere moth // entombed // among catacombs, // To the flame // I plunge, // Phoenix and Mantis, // mating eagles to doves // speaks volumes. I have had an "eagle" synchronicity recently (cr: attached "chit-chat II" with eagle note... I wish you could have been there but I know you and Janet were on a mission).

Plus, the juxtaposition: Caesars, // prostitutes of Yaldobaoth // I am – // honesty, // humanity's birthright, // the fool // who employed // Lucifer... // } Don't worry Rick – you woke up; besides, as you said later: you are doomed to perfection.

Your brilliance really comes to the fore with *THE HORSEMEN COMETH*. I loved just about everything in this section... for example, the whole of *Xenophobic* is a masterpiece: // a forbidden planet, // } How apt an expression a la Melville's ocean ruled by Moby Dick. // your agendas filling // Mother's breast // } My mother god damn it!!! // with snapped bones, // skeletons // of her children // } Magnificent! // How natural // your grin // upon the infant's // chain addiction // } Boy, did you nail the imagery here. // talons of the // global oppression // The gridlock of Marshall Law // } Armies of Darkness... yes, yes, yes – who are about to try to crush me via IRS lien on my salary. :(// chain not my vision // not my spirit // } Amen Rick!

Note: I had a synchronicity while reading *Sexism* on phrase // Eye to eye //; I heard on my audio tape Clannad (of which I had several synchronicities). It was the phrase "close my eyes" [Time 9:06am on Nov. 17th]. Maybe your eyes are now budding to open before they blossom to full gnosis since you need to wring out the necessary fertilizer and wash yourself until you are fully clean... allusion from tractate before "Book of Thomas, the Contender" (cr: p.194 in the Nag Hammadi, "Exegesis of the Soul"). Believe me, I was guided to the page

116

since I only remember the simile – not where it was – guided divinely because this was an important statement in the Nag Hammadi. Meditate on...

I liked the way you referenced Enki and Enlil** in *Nationalist* as the twins of Arrogance and Chauvinism } These were our parental links?!? No wonder the Kingdom of Man is all screwed up! (**inferred by David Icke as reptiles in The Biggest Secret and therefore criticizes Sitchin for not going far enough.) :(

Wouldn't it be interesting if the "Mother" you were linked to is the very insect-like ones alluded to by Karla Turner in *Into The Fringe*, now looking to overcome the Patriarchy of Reptiles?!? Thought for the day...

*****

So I see your poetry as a reflection of Total Reality, reflected beautifully in *My Accusers* where: To my right, // Sitchin... godfather, // } Curious imagery.
// my left, // Sagan... laughingstock, // } Nag Hammadi references... Testimony of Truth... 2nd Treatise of Great Seth.
// in front, // a sea of riots // (Note: Sagan = Nagas; another John the Baptist controlling Jordan flow of knowledge.) Your poetry is sending me to other levels, like *The Back Left Corner of Heaven* – I loved this poem – yet Death brings New Life. :)

Lastly, my other favorite – *Genetic Legacy* – as part of the whole fittingly called *INTO THE FRINGE*. The // English Ivy // } spreading like the horn of the Heifer of Ephram... the Manifest Destiny of the Kingdom of Man (cr: the Evolution of Israel by deWelden and 'chit-chat I' at MUFON).
// the Mantis, // her seeds laid // in lush pastures // } ready to bud the blossom.
// starborne healers // of biological evolution // } Cool... real cool!

*****

117

Rick Smith

My epilogue to Rick;

Your brilliance as an artist/poet may only be outweighed by a remark
from Shakespeare [enlightened Freemason, blue-blooded nobleman of
suspicious origin]:
"He loved not wisely but too well…"

In short Rick, hopefully you have been fully christened into new
awareness so now the Butterfly of your Essence will fully emerge – I
know you will do it!

Love from your good friend
with a Rebel's Righteousness,
byron lebeau

BULLdog Productions
http://hey_223.tripod.com/thebudtheblossom/

Expressing the Abduction Phenomena
An interview with Rick Smith, painter and poet

by Joan Carra
January, 2003

I met Rick Smith, at the **UFO Arts Festival** *in NYC. It was a multi-media event that presented lecturers, painters, musicians and poets expressing the pain, bewilderment and excitement of the abduction experience. These weren't sci-fi enthusiasts, but people who had actual terrifying experiences. The* **N.Y. Times** *even did a two-page report on this budding arts' movement. Three galleries were devoting shows to this theme and musicians and poets were performing.*

I was both M.C. of the event and a veteran performing UFO poetry. Rick Smith, at the time, a fine arts student at **SUNY College**, *lectured and presented his artwork, which was both intense and passionate. His technique and message displayed maturity and insight beyond his age. Rick Smith's paintings explore, confront and question the unexplained with pained honesty.*

As with his artwork as a painter, Rick expresses with his poetry profound lessons and insights with multidimensional metaphors. His candor shows true courage and imagination. How do you possibly put into perspective "extraterrestrialism" – encounters beyond the realm of earthly expectations, encounters beyond sanity?

My Starchild, My Daughter (a message)

excerpt:

between the sheets
of mated lovers,
within twilight's night,
a paranormal calling
met our wanton desires

Starchild,
glow of our life,
you and your siblings,
seedlings
of the interstellar

Rick Smith

Rick is a father but not here on earth. He has a hybrid daughter. His psyche is an astronaut without prescient.

When did you first start to paint the extraterrestrial experience?

During the year-long hiatus from school, I had turned 21 (Dec.'91) – and this is when my first awakening came with regard to the Abduction Phenomena. It served as a motivational tool for attending the Visual Arts curriculum at Old Westbury. The awakening brought back all of the 'contact' experiences I had as a child, but passed off as only a dream/nightmare during my childhood. It was a clusterbomb of memories that flooded back into me. At that point all things became clear as to what had been in my past and what direction I would be going in for the future. Basically, I was asked if I would use my talents and skills as an artist to educate the masses via visual communication as a teacher.

With that came the agreement that I would receive downloaded information from an entity I refer to in my book **Legions of Light / Armies of Darkness** as "Mother." This information would then be translated into the artwork. From that point on (Spring, 1993), my career as an artist became dedicated to Extraterrestrial Intervention. The book, published in October 1999, serves as a parallel to the artwork. As it turns out, my extraterrestrial guide – Mother (a.k.a. the Crone) – has always been there since the day I was born.

One of his college professors, Luis Camnitzer, was a strong influence on inspiring Rick to explore the social and political aspects of the UFO phenomena. Camnitzer's own work is recognized internationally as a provocative and controversial artist. His mentoring allowed Rick "the freedom to aggressively focus on exploring the Abduction Phenomena" in the confines of academia's strict protocols.

I don't think he ever believed a damn thing I said. However, he may have been able to appreciate it from a political standpoint, understanding the social ramifications it would have on global issues concerning civil rights. The reason I say this is that his own work had already been dealing with controversial and historical subject matter regarding the human condition. So it seems logical that this may have served as the common thread.

It was brand spankin' new on the cutting edge of an unexplored frontier that enveloped all social, political and historical issues at once! It became quite apparent as to where I was going with this and that I wasn't screwing around. As time went on, the artwork became much more aggressive and experimental, graduating from acrylics to mixed-media to installation work. Once again, my obsessive, relentless, dedicated nature from commercial art kicked in as I had a new venue for applying it right on up to my final Senior Exhibition (first solo exhibition). After I had graduated from Old Westbury College (1996), the name 'UFOteacher' was born.

Why are you drawn to the UFO subject?

I was born into it. It's a genealogical phenomenon that follows the descendants of a bloodline. In many cases, those bloodlines lead directly back to an original extraterrestrial presence during the Old Kingdom of Egypt. There is nothing nice about this realization as the Egyptian Empire represents the most aggressive slave campaign against the human race during the last Patriarchal invasion.

You call yourself UFOteacher; do you feel this is your mission?

Definitely. I am a highly driven artist involved with and dedicated to the Abduction Phenomena and extraterrestrial intervention - which is *the* tantamount global, political, social, cultural, personal and historical issue all Americans should be striving to educate themselves on. I believe that my fellow human beings have put up with enough lies and deceptions and they deserve better, they deserve truth and honesty in a Constitutional Democracy.

In Rick's own words he explains one of his first Abduction Paintings – *Destiny of a legacy: in the beginning.*

121

Rick Smith

It focuses on the three main kingdoms of Earth being depicted as prisms or test tube experiments: sea, air and land. The three kingdoms are represented as a Blue Whale, an American Bald Eagle and the union of a human sperm and egg cell with the daisy blossoming as the flower of life. The symbolisms all work on multiple levels. The kingdoms of sea and air are completed in their form, finished with majestic creatures that have also been on the endangered species list due to the human race's selective ignorance. The kingdom of land remains unfinished, a haunting reminder that we are in an incomplete form, with an end result that remains undefined due to the influence of our own extraterrestrial progenitors. One such progenitor is camouflaged in the background, overseeing all of this as a very shady God.

What artists do you admire?

Anyone who makes a dent in the Arts and survives the onslaught of that tired old patriarchal abattoir called His-Story deserves to be admired. As for actual names, there are too many to list here. However, the two that tend to come out on top are Peter Paul Rubens and Salvador Dali.

One can see the classical draftsmanship of Peter Paul Ruebens and the Surreal nightmares of Dali in Rick's unusual expression of interdimensional trauma and intrigue. Welcome to a brave new world, which now incorporates Mother Earth and her friends and fiends in the outer limits of the galaxy.

His paintings are on display at his website gallery www.UFOteacher.com You can also purchase his book there **Legions of Light/Armies of Darkness** as well.

Joan Carra
http://members.aol.com/JORDANIA12/

When Extraterrestrials Try To Decipher Email
or
Why 'They' Do Not Talk To Us
by Rick Smith
Last Tuesday

It has come to my attention that there are a lot of imbeciles in the world today.

These mental waifs are the type that keep asking the same damn ignorant questions over and over:

Q: Why don't the aliens talk to us?
A: You have to be a shmuck to ask this question - now put yourself in their shoes.

Q: When are they going to come down here?
A: Let's see... fictitious president... never elected... social fad called democracy... never meant to work... and you still remain in denial on that one. Fictitious wars to satisfy your Feudal economic slavemasters... and they in turn satisfy the profit margins of their own non-indigenous masters from afar. *Why in hell should they come down here?!?*

As long as things remain in this happy state of pure el crap-a-mundo, there is no reason for them to come down here and communicate with the slaves. Their own robber barons and carpetbaggers – one being that mongoloid prick you call a president – are doing a great job. The operation has been a success.

Q: But aren't there any good ones?
A: I wouldn't be here if there weren't, sugar-bumps. However, try to remember that 'as it is above so it is below.' Translation: the bureaucratic mentality is the only constant in the universe.
                                                    – *Dr. Leonard "Bones" McCoy*

Q: How can we talk to them?
A: You are talking to one of them now. Disappointed? Don't worry. I am feeling really generous today so I am going to elaborate here with an essay I recently wrote. You see, there are three main markers used to

123

Rick Smith

establish and measure the worth of a particular global society or race of people, as well as its potential for direct communication:

     1. the homeless and poverty stricken
     2. the traditional crap you raise your kids on
     3. junk email

As you can see, these three social markers also happen to be the three most common telltale denominators of any global society. They pretty much cover all the bases. I am sure that if you take stock of all three listed above, you will be able to answer your own questions about the good, the bad and the ugly who come from afar.

In case the third one seems a little obscure to some of you, please feel free to read my essay below. I am sure it will explain quite a bit. It was extracted directly from my junk email subject lines. As a favor to all of you reading this, I strung them together in sentence format – one right after the other – with no commercial interruptions!

As you read this little etude, try to understand it from their perspective. Imagine one of them looking over your shoulder as you are reading the subject lines to your inbox of new messages.

*****

When Extraterrestrials Try To Decipher Email
or
Why 'They' Do Not Talk To Us

Hey, would you like to travel safely with an Impressively Rock Hard "resume"? We can get you out of debt with these hardcore videos of Paul Gauguin. 100 years later, the Centenary of his Death means cheaper sex – It's That SIMPLE!!

With these amazing naked pictures you can see why some people are fat as chicks without clothes share the secrets of Online Auctions.

Joining the LEADERS will give you what you are looking for with Shaved blondes who are Bent Over your Ebay's Registration Data as you End All Your Debts. Regain financial stability with our live Fantasy girls at the adult mega site where one does it all for Wild dirty teens with added job options and wealthy prospects!

Need to spice up your love life? Get one now with ENCOURAGED MEMBERS who are A Joy To Everyone as college girls go naked with All Major Credit Cards!!

Act now and join all nine adult sites for free with your Express Merchant Account. Amazing naked girls Melt Body Fat Away with the Lowest Rates In 30 Years! Join a dirty site for larger hoes where Naked pictures Of me are posted with a Digital Camera On A Keychain – yours for only $39.95 – while Dorm amateurs Get Her Excited With Your Big NOKIA CELLPHONE OFFER.

So Be A HERO, Perform In The BEDROOM and Have Her Choking On Medical problems destroying your life, as we give you FreeShipping + $50 Cash for every Long Distance Bill that These girls swallow. We can get you out of debt with these SEDUCTIVE PHEROMONES that Look 10 Years Younger Guaranteed!

Remember, Twins Get Reamed Hard with Digital Cameras On a Special Offer At a Free Smut Session – so pick up the certificate without wasting the Subscription offer.

Experience beautiful women who crave your changing member proportions as you Encounter Devoted And Appreciative Women, Kinky teens, Free lezbos and the American Minimalist – Donald Judd! Artprice Basics offers More pussy than you can shake a "stick" at with Extreme Discounts on UFO videos, Hot love pics and a Cool university degree proposition.

But remember, you can change and Get Cash Now For Anything With No Credit Check at the hottest site on the net featuring secret love kittens just for me. Don't you Wish You Were Making Money With Your Vacation?

Rick Smith

It's not too late to get Mom's gift with the best selling prescriptions as Your Job Leads SLASH YOUR BILLS BY 50% INSTANTLY! I found this to be the only way out of my newest movie "*High Mortgage, NO LOANS, Your Manhood and Apple Cider.*" So Market Your Resume & GET HIRED as Ashley makes certain of how we save up to 70% over car dealers with No aggravation from instant vehicle quotes online. HURRY! The she-males are waiting for you.

Looking for a Hot date? If it smacks of Rapid Fire, don't worry – I did my research so that you can Create a Better Life for Yourself Today. Why Wait? Stay Young Forever and REGAIN CONTROL OF YOUR FAMILIES FINANCES with these Iraqi game cards as seen on nightly news – part man and part woman. A Millionaire will Pay You For Giving Away His Loot with Women who talk about sex as much as men! So Use Viagra and get a NEW eMac – NOW up to 1.0 GHz – and Lose 10 pounds fast!

Hurry! Chocolate Sale ends Friday, May 16, with The Profile You Submitted at Disney World and MGM Studios. Gamers are Wanted for the Ultimate Fat Burner – the Fat Assassin Kit! Receive your Delivery Status Notification and Discover The Secrets To Profits Online while Earning Extra Income and Increasing your breast size without surgery.

Dear Madame, This May Be Your Job as Your Resume Particulars are so simple that we could feasibly give you 70 percent off the combined retail value of an ULTIMATE DVD Combo! Save $20.00 on A Giveaway Vacation – No Bull!

Let me help you learn and earn income with a Free Trial of Human Growth Hormone. Save $49.00 and Avoid public disclosure at a Career Event in your Area with a 60% BILL REDUCTION. Get Ready to Be Hired as California Revokes Wells Fargo's Mortgage Lending in a Special VIP Invitation from EVERY Apple Computer.

Dirty girl pictures of itty bitty titties on Big butt models can make you Look 21 Again Through Our Assistance. The results will amaze you with Free No Repay Cash Grants, Up To $50,000 while supplies last.

126